The Job of a CIVIC LEADER

Attorney General

Stephanie Gaston

Table of Contents

A Starfish Book

SEAHORSE PUBLISHING

Teaching Tips for Caregivers:

As a caregiver, you can help your child succeed in school by giving them a strong foundation in language and literacy skills and a desire to learn to read.

This book helps children grow by letting them practice reading skills.

Reading for pleasure and interest will help your child to develop reading skills and will give your child the opportunity to practice these skills in meaningful ways.

- Encourage your child to read on her own at home
- Encourage your child to practice reading aloud
- Encourage activities that require reading
- Establish a reading time
- Talk with your child
- Give your child writing materials

Teaching Tips for Teachers:

Research shows that one of the best ways for students to learn a new topic is to read about it.

Before Reading

- Read the "Words to Know" and discuss the meaning of each word.
- Read the back cover to see what the book is about.

During Reading

- When a student gets to a word that is unknown, ask them to look at the rest of the sentence to find clues to help with the meaning of the unknown word.
- Ask the student to write down any pages of the book that were confusing to them.

After Reading

- Discuss the main idea of the book.
- Ask students to give one detail that they learned in the book by showing a text dependent answer from the book.

Attorney General

The Attorney General is the top **lawyer** in the **government** of the United States.

Alberto R. Gonzales
80th Attorney General
of the United States

George W. Bush
43rd President
of the United States

The President picks the
U.S. Attorney General.

The **Senate** must approve the President's choice.

The U.S. Attorney General is a member of the President's **cabinet**.

The U.S. Attorney General helps the President understand laws and carry them out.

The U.S. Attorney General also leads the **Department of Justice**.

DEPARTMENT
OF
JUSTICE

Merrick Garland became the U.S. Attorney General in 2021.

He was chosen by President Joe Biden.

Merrick Garland
86th Attorney General of the United States

Joe Biden
46th President of the United States

Janet Reno was the first woman U.S. Attorney General.

Eric Holder was the first African American U.S. Attorney General.

Loretta Lynch became the first African American woman to have the job.

Janet Reno
78th Attorney General
of the United States

Eric Holder
82nd Attorney General
of the United States

Loretta Lynch
83rd Attorney General
of the United States

Each state in the United States has its own Attorney General.

In some states, people vote for the Attorney General.

In other states, the Governor picks the Attorney General.

State Attorneys General help make sure that people are following the laws of the state.

They can also suggest ideas for new laws.

In 38 states, the law says that the Attorney General must be a U.S. **citizen**.

In 43 states, the law says that the Attorney General must live in the state.

In 35 states, the law says that the Attorney General must be a certain age.

In 25 states, the law says that the Attorney General can keep the job for only four years at a time.

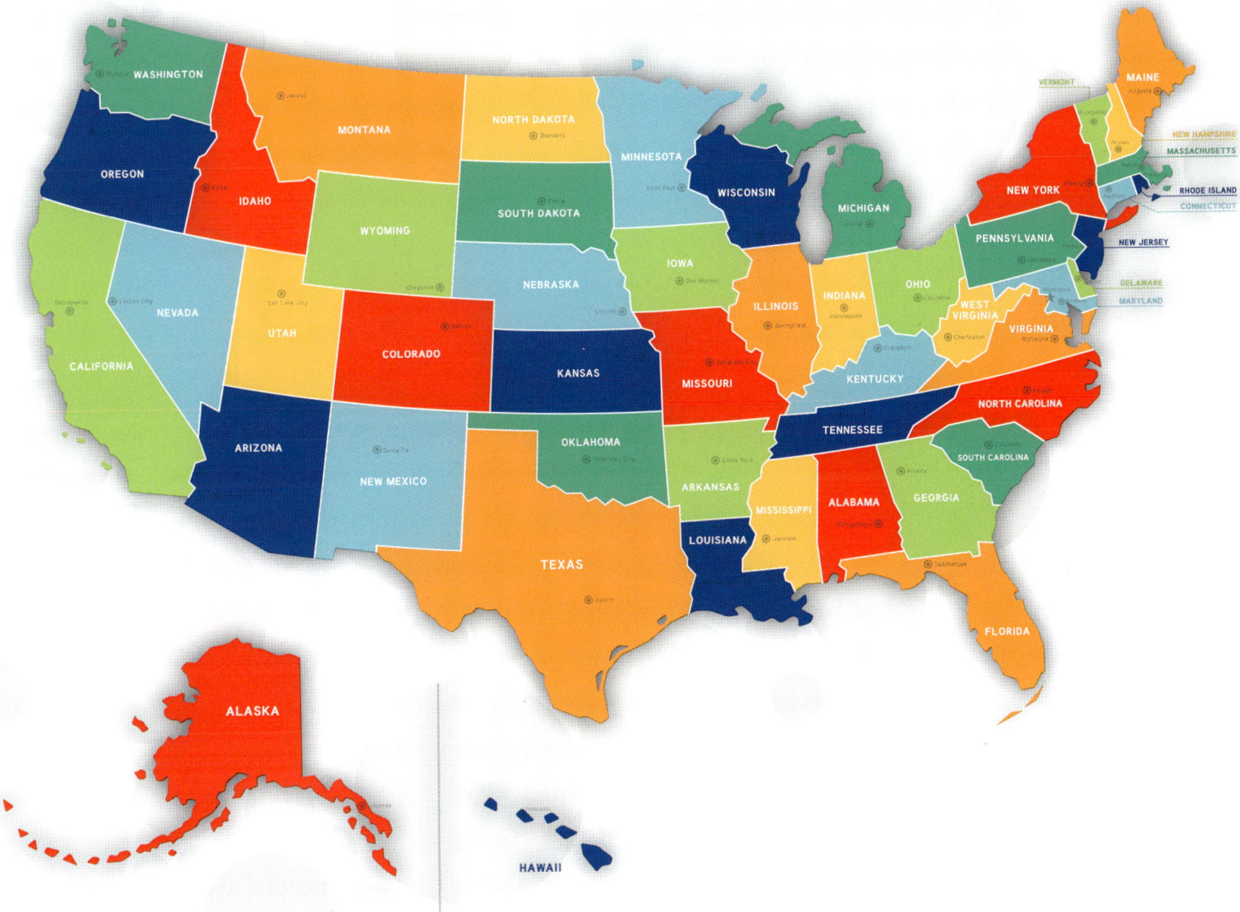
WASHINGTON
OREGON
CALIFORNIA
IDAHO
NEVADA
MONTANA
WYOMING
UTAH
ARIZONA
COLORADO
NEW MEXICO
NORTH DAKOTA
SOUTH DAKOTA
NEBRASKA
KANSAS
OKLAHOMA
TEXAS
MINNESOTA
IOWA
MISSOURI
ARKANSAS
LOUISIANA
WISCONSIN
ILLINOIS
MICHIGAN
INDIANA
OHIO
KENTUCKY
TENNESSEE
MISSISSIPPI
ALABAMA
GEORGIA
FLORIDA
SOUTH CAROLINA
NORTH CAROLINA
VIRGINIA
WEST VIRGINIA
PENNSYLVANIA
NEW YORK
VERMONT
MAINE
NEW HAMPSHIRE
MASSACHUSETTS
RHODE ISLAND
CONNECTICUT
NEW JERSEY
DELAWARE
MARYLAND
ALASKA
HAWAII

Vice President Kamala Harris was the Attorney General for the state of California.

She had the job from 2011 to 2017.

Kamala Harris
32nd Attorney General of the state of California

The Attorney General has an important job.

This leader helps people understand and follow the law.

Words to Know

cabinet (KAB-uh-nit): a group of advisers for the head of a government; the cabinet helps the leader of a country or a state make decisions

citizen (SIT-i-zuhn): a person who has the full rights of a country such as the right to live there, work there, and vote in its elections

Department of Justice (di-PAHRT-muhnt uhv JUHS-tis): a main part of the national government of the United States that has the responsibility of enforcing laws

government (GUHV-urn-muhnt): the system by which a country, state, or other organization is run; the group of people who govern

lawyer (LAW-yur): a person whose job is to represent people or governments in a court of law and to give advice about the law

Senate (SEN-it): one of the two houses of the U.S. Congress that make laws; each state has two Senators

Index

Comprehension Questions

1. Who chooses the U.S. Attorney General?
   a. the Senate
   b. the President
   c. the Vice President

2. The U.S. Attorney General is a member of _____.
   a. the President's cabinet
   b. the Senate
   c. the state of California

3. **True or False:** There is an Attorney General in all 50 states.

4. **True or False:** Janet Reno was chosen by President Joe Biden.

5. **True or False:** The state Attorney General can suggest new laws.

Answers 1. b 2. a 3. True 4. False 5. True

About the Author

Stephanie Gaston is a journalist who has covered major stories including presidential inaugurations, natural disasters, and royal weddings. She has spent over a decade working in news for both local and major networks like CNN. Stephanie is a first-generation Haitian-American who grew up in Ft. Lauderdale, FL, a diverse community with Latin and Caribbean influences. In addition to being a writer, Stephanie is a dog lover, movie buff, fitness enthusiast, and most importantly, a proud mom.

Written by: Stephanie Gaston
Design by: Jen Bowers
Editor: Kim Thompson

Library of Congress PCN Data
Attorney General / Stephanie Gaston
The Job of a Civic Leader
ISBN 978-1-6389-7966-1 (hard cover)
ISBN 979-8-8873-5025-7 (paperback)
ISBN 979-8-8873-5084-4 (EPUB)
ISBN 979-8-8873-5143-8 (eBook)
Library of Congress Control Number: 2022942009

Printed in the United States of America.

Photographs/Shutterstock: Cover and interior background circles © magic pictures, cover images ©2018 create jobs 51, ©2019 MDart10; p.3 legal pad ©2013 Mega Pixel, ©2013 StudioSmart; p.4 Public Domain/United States Department of Justice, ©2012 Northfoto; p.5 ©2016 Rob Crandall; p.7 ©2019 MDart10; p.9 Public Domain/United States Department of Justice, Public Domain/Official White House Photo/Adam Schultz; p.11 ©2018 mark reinstein, Public Domain/United States Department of Justice; p.12 ©2017 EQRoy; p.13 ©2016 AntonSokolov; p.14 © vectorplus; p.15 ©2022 Pickadook; p.17 © Fourleaflover; p.19 Public Domain/Official White House Photo/Lawrence Jackson; p.21 ©2021 Supavadee butradee

Seahorse Publishing Company
www.seahorsepub.com

Published in the United States
Seahorse Publishing
PO Box 771325
Coral Springs, FL 33077

SEAHORSE PUBLISHING